Genius Cat Books

A Business of Ferrets

Collective Nouns of the Animal Kingdom

Written and Illustrated by
Lauren Beckwith

For Levi and Isaac

You've probably heard
of a **pack** of wolves,

A litter
of kittens,

or cattle in a **drove.**

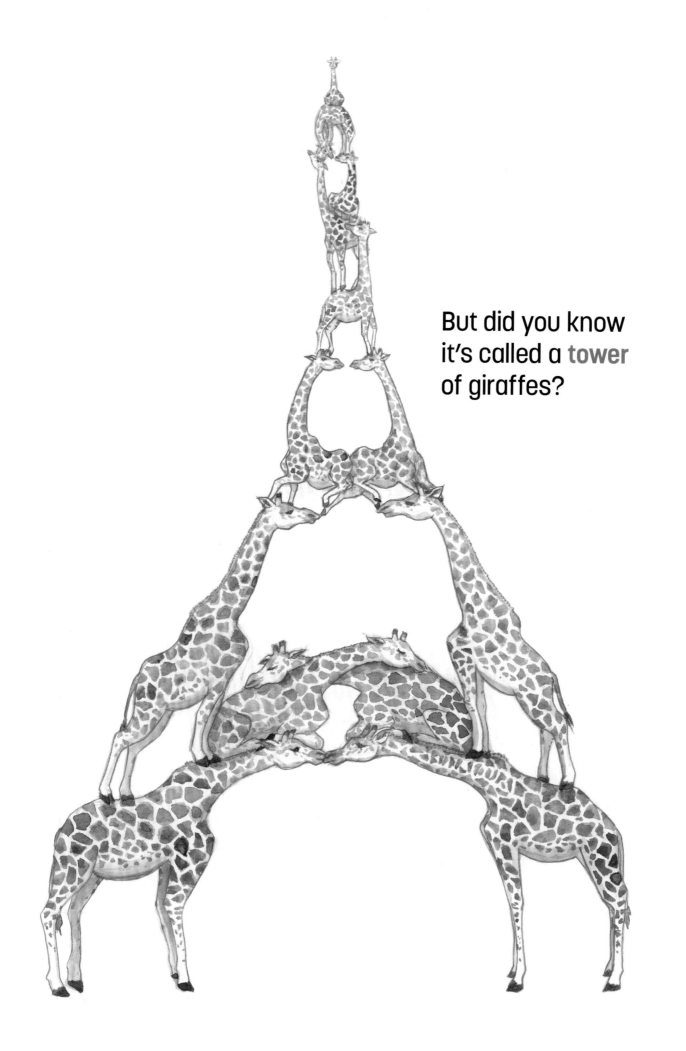

But did you know
it's called a **tower**
of giraffes?

A **bloat** of hippos?

A **wisdom** of wombats?

Watch out for the
crash of rhinos

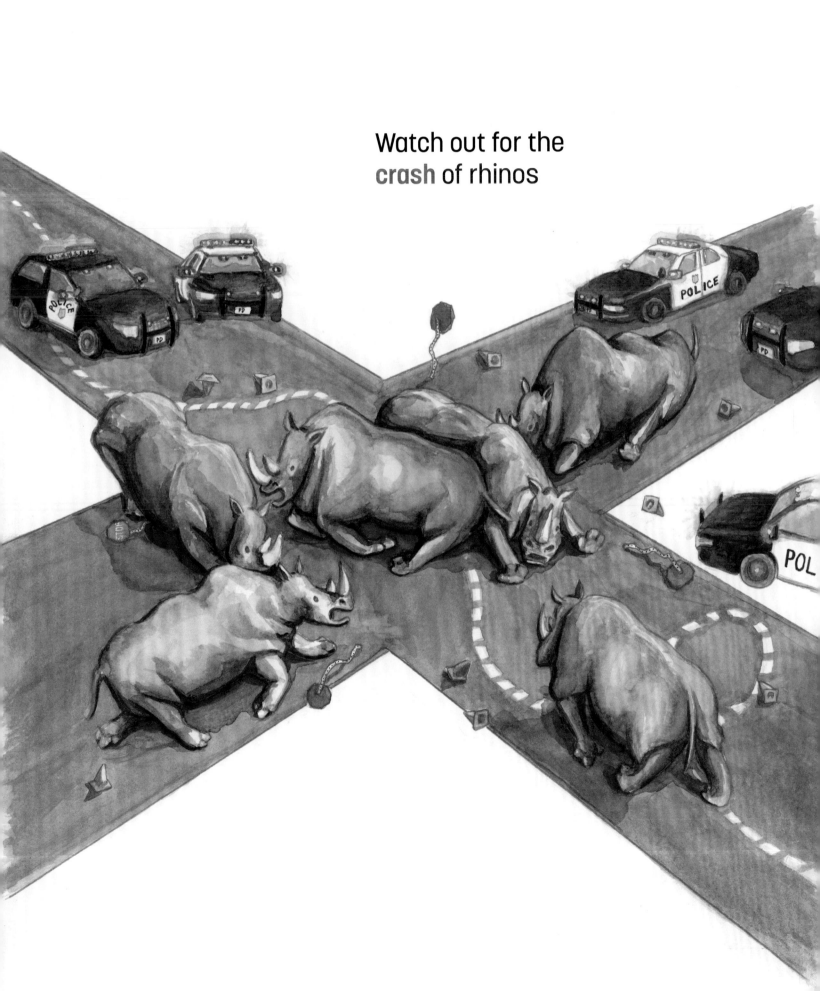

and the tigers —
away they **streak**!

Hear the cackle of hyenas?
Just listen for the shriek!

If you're looking for friends,
consider a mischief of mice

or a **knot** of
colorful snakes.

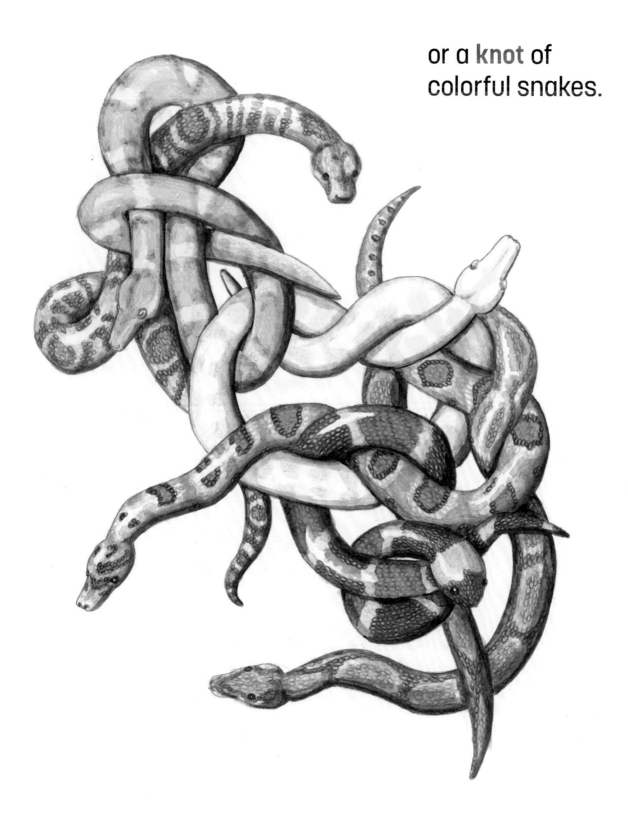

Maybe you'd prefer a business of ferrets.

But be careful!
They like to escape.

Solve a crime with a **sleuth** of bears

and march with an
army of frogs!

Count the butterflies in their **kaleidoscope**

Join the wise owls of **parliament**,

or play along with a
band of gorillas!

If you want to get a little dizzy,
join the **roll** of armadillos!

Slippery penguins
form a **convent**,

and an **eclipse** is for the moths.

Walruses collect in a **pod**,

while a bed is dreamy with sloths.

If you're having trouble falling asleep,

you might try counting a fold of sheep.

Or number the leopards
soaring overhead —

that's why they're called a **leap**.

Thanks for reading along!

I bet you learned
something new.

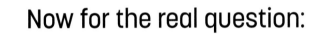

Now for the real question:

what should we call
a group of you?

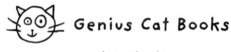

Genius Cat Books

www.geniuscatbooks.com
Parkland, FL

ABOUT THIS BOOK
The art for this book was created with pencils and watercolors edited with photoshop and illustrator, using a Wacom Cintiq. Text was set in Chaloops and Korolev. It was designed by Germán Blanco.

Library of Congress Control Number: 2022935086

ISBN: -978-1-938447-50-1 (hardcover)

First edition, 2022

Our books may be purchased in bulk for promotional, educational, or business use. For more information, or to schedule an event, please visit geniuscatbooks.com.

Printed and bound in China.